Daylight Moonlight

Matt Patterson

Schiffer Publishing Ltd®

4880 Lower Valley Road • Atglen, PA 19310

Other Schiffer Books on Related Subjects:

In Mouse's Backyard. James Nardi. ISBN: 978-0-7643-3833-5. $16.99
Mother Monarch. Mindy Lighthipe. ISBN: 978-0-7643-3400-9. $19.99

Type set in Souvenir Lt BT/Souvenir Lt BT

ISBN: 978-0-7643-4282-0
Printed in China

Published by Schiffer Publishing, Ltd.
4880 Lower Valley Road
Atglen, PA 19310
Phone: (610) 593-1777; Fax: (610) 593-2002
E-mail: Info@schifferbooks.com

For the largest selection of fine reference books on this and related subjects, please visit our website at **www.schifferbooks.com.** You may also write for a free catalog.

This book may be purchased from the publisher.
Please try your bookstore first.

We are always looking for people to write books on new and related subjects. If you have an idea for a book, please contact us at proposals@schifferbooks.com

Schiffer Books are available at special discounts for bulk purchases for sales promotions or premiums. Special editions, including personalized covers, corporate imprints, and excerpts can be created in large quantities for special needs. For more information contact the publisher.

In Europe, Schiffer books are distributed by
Bushwood Books
6 Marksbury Ave.
Kew Gardens
Surrey TW9 4JF England
Phone: 44 (0) 20 8392 8585; Fax: 44 (0) 20 8392 9876
E-mail: info@bushwoodbooks.co.uk
Website: www.bushwoodbooks.co.uk

Dedication

This book is dedicated to my mother, Ann Patterson.

Desert

In the desert, the sun is bright during the day. As the sun shines, a desert tortoise searches for grass to eat.

At night, an owl emerges from his cactus nest and a ringtail, at home in the dark, crawls over the desert rocks in search of food.

Pond

A painted turtle and water snake share a rock on the pond's edge catching the warm rays of the sun.

Spring peepers fill the night with their soothing songs.

Florida

In the forest of Florida, a panther rests in the shade and a lizard shows off his red crest while on the trunk of a tree.

Cubs of a mother black bear play in a tree while a pair of barn owls watch from above.

Underwater

Underwater, a mudpuppy rests on a weed while a frog swims for his life, trying to escape from a hungry bass!

At night, catfish with their long whiskers sense their way through the dark.

Coast

Whales and dolphins jump from the water offshore.
On the beach, a seal rests in the warm sun.

A raccoon comes out at night to scavenge for food and two horseshoe crabs crawl onto the shore.

City

The city park is a busy place during the day. Children are playing soccer, dogs are being walked, and pigeons are searching for crumbs of food.

An owl flies through the night sky while two stray cats prowl on the ground.

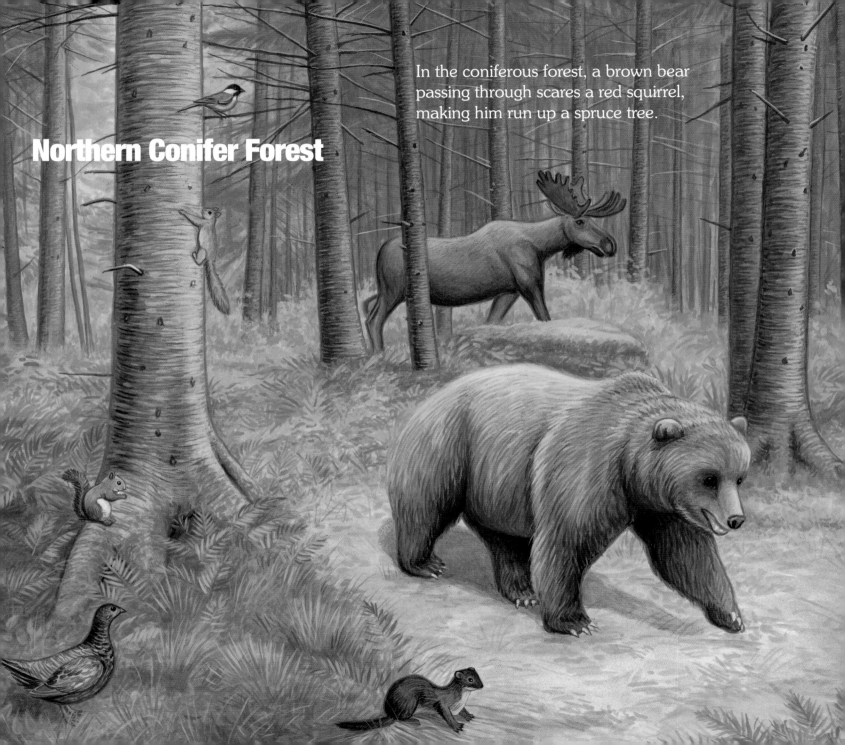

Northern Conifer Forest

In the coniferous forest, a brown bear passing through scares a red squirrel, making him run up a spruce tree.

A flying squirrel, with large eyes to see in the dark, jumps above from the branches.

Redwood

The normally large looking elk seems small compared to the giant redwood trees.

The trees are home to
owls and bobcats that
come out at night.

Backyard

Two dogs rest from playing while chickens roam free in the yard.

At night, an owl lands on the roof and a lunar moth flies through the crisp air.

Buffalo, often in huge herds, graze on the prairie grass along with elk and pronghorn.

Prairie

A wolf howls at the moon as his pack runs behind him. Soon the night will end and a new day will begin.

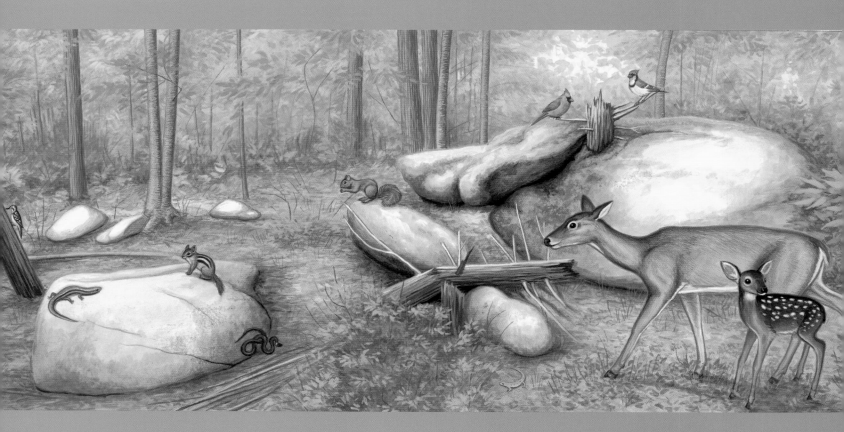

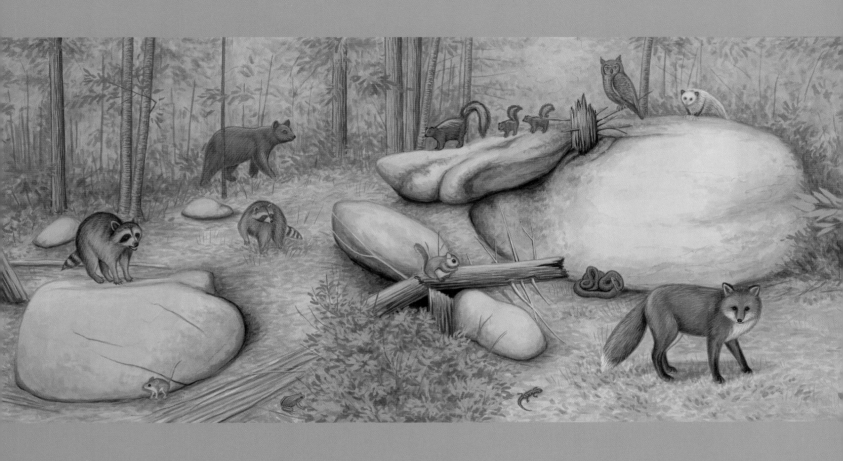

Desert

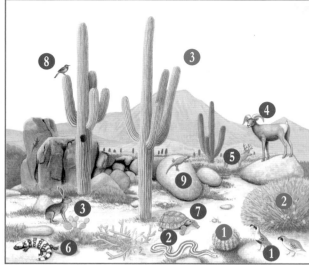

1. Gambel's Quail
2. Mexican Rosy Boa
3. Antelope Jackrabbit
4. Desert Bighorn
5. Mule Deer
6. Gila Monster
7. Desert Tortoise
8. Cactus Wren
9. Chuckwalla
10. Burrowing Owl
11. Coyote
12. Western Spotted Skunk
13. Ringtail
14. Sonora Sidewinder
15. Desert Tarantula
16. Bark Scorpion
17. Collared Peccaries
18. Bats

Plants

1. Barrel Cactus
2. Brittle Bush
3. Saguaro Cactus

Pond

1. Canada Goose
2. Largemouth Bass
3. Wood Duck
4. Eastern Painted Turtle
5. Northern Water Snake
6. Moose
7. Blue Heron
8. Beaver
9. Dragonfly
10. Red-winged Blackbird
11. Bullfrog
12. Muskrat
13. Otter
14. Leopard Frog
15. Spring Peeper
16. Mink
17. Gray Treefrog
18. Bank Swallow
19. Mallard

Plants

1. Cattails

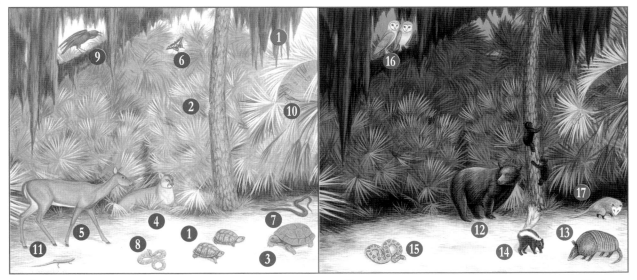

Florida

① Florida Box Turtle	⑦ Eastern Indigo Snake	⑫ Black Bear	⑯ Barn Owl	*Plants*
② Green Anole	⑧ Corn Snake	⑬ Armadillo	⑰ Possum	① Spanish Moss
③ Gopher Tortoise	⑨ American Crow	⑭ Skunk		
④ Florida Panther	⑩ Mocking Bird	⑮ Eastern Diamondback		
⑤ White Tailed Deer	⑪ Southern Five-lined Skink			
⑥ Giant Swallowtail				

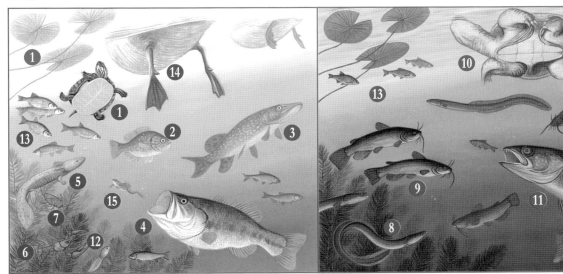

Underwater

① Eastern Painted Turtle	⑤ Mudpuppy	⑧ American Eel	⑫ Bullfrog Tadpole	*Plants*
② Pumpkinseed Sunfish	⑥ Crayfish	⑨ Brown Bullhead	⑬ Golden Shiner	① Lilly pad
③ Northern Pike	⑦ Giant Water Beetle	⑩ Snapping Turtle	⑭ Ducks	
④ Largemouth Bass		⑪ Walleye	⑮ Frog	

Coast

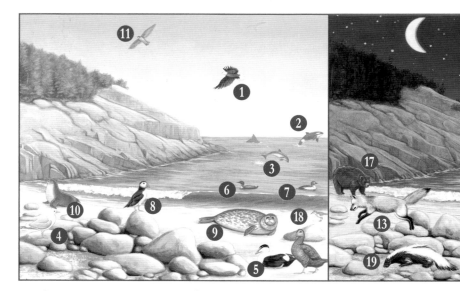

1. Bald Eagle
2. Killer Whale
3. Bottlenose Dolphin
4. Seagull
5. Common Eiders
6. Loon
7. Common Goldeneye
8. Puffin
9. Harbor Seal
10. Sea Lion
11. Peregrine Falcon
12. Raccoon
13. Red Fox
14. Horseshoe Crab
15. Humpback Whale
16. Otter
17. Black Bear
18. Sandpiper
19. Skunk

City

1. Red-tailed Hawk
2. Pigeon
3. Monarch Butterfly
4. Cottontail Rabbit
5. Raccoon
6. Skunk
7. Rat
8. Possum
9. Great Horned Owl

Northern Conifer Forest

1. Moose
2. Brown Bear
3. Spruce Grouse
4. Red Squirrel
5. Chickadee
6. Short Tailed Weasel
7. Great Horned Owl
8. Bobcat
9. Raccoon
10. Porcupine
11. Red Fox
12. Timber Wolf
13. Flying Squirrel
14. Western Toad

Redwood

1. Bald Eagle
2. Stellar Jay
3. Western Grey Squirrel
4. American Marten
5. Black Tailed Deer
6. Roosevelt Elk
7. Black Bear
8. Gray Fox
9. Bobcat
10. Mountain Lion
11. Raccoon
12. Northern Spotted Owl

Plants
1. Giant Redwood Tree

Backyard

① American Toad	⑤ Garter Snake	⑨ Raccoon	⑫ Grey Squirrel
② Cottontail Rabbit	⑥ Lunar Moth	⑩ Barn Owl	⑬ Rooster
③ Blue Jay	⑦ Skunk	⑪ Possum	⑭ Hens
④ Northern Cardinal	⑧ Red Fox		

Prairie

① Prairie Dog	⑥ Swift Fox	⑩ Coyote	⑬ Black Footed Ferret
② American Bison	⑦ Jackrabbit	⑪ American Badger	⑭ Short-eared Owl
③ Pronghorn	⑧ Red Tailed Hawk	⑫ Gray Wolf	⑮ Western Rattlesnake
④ Elk	⑨ Gopher Snake		⑯ Bats
⑤ Tiger Swallowtail Butterfly			

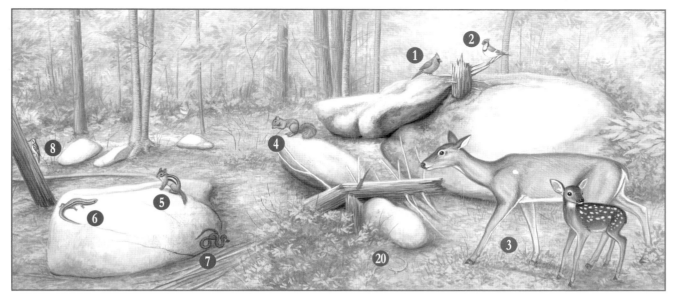

1. Northern Cardinal
2. Blue Jay
3. White-tailed Deer
4. Grey Squirrel
5. Chipmunk
6. Coal Skink
7. Ring-necked Snake
8. Downy Woodpecker

9. Possum
10. Black Bear
11. Red Fox
12. Flying Squirrel
13. Raccoon
14. Wood Frog
15. Yellow Spotted Salamander
16. Great Horned Owl
17. Deer Mouse
18. Rat Snake
19. Skunks
20. Orange Newt